Helping Children See Jesus

ISBN: 978-1-64104-003-7

Joseph Part 2
Old Testament Volume 5:
Genesis Part 5

Author: Arlene Piepgrass
Illustrator: Vernon Henkel
Computer Graphic Artist: Andrew Cross
Typesetting and Layout: Morgan Melton, Patricia Pope

© 2018 Bible Visuals International
PO Box 153, Akron, PA 17501-0153
Phone: (717) 859-1131
www.biblevisuals.org

All rights reserved. No part of this publication may be reproduced, stored in a retrieval system or transmitted in any form by any means, electronic, mechanical, photocopy, recording or otherwise, without the prior permission of the publisher, except as provided by USA copyright law.

RELATED ITEMS

To access related items (such as activities, memory verse posters and translated texts) please visit our web store at shop.biblevisuals.org and enter 2005 in the search box on the page.

FREE TEXT DOWNLOAD

To access a FREE printable copy of the teaching text (PDF format) in English or other available languages, enter S2005DL in the search box. Add the item to your cart, and use coupon code XTACSV17 at checkout. Once your order is processed you will receive an email with a link to the free download.

We know that all things work together for good to them that love God. — Romans 8:28a

Lesson 1
TRIALS IN EGYPT (Part 1)

Scripture to be studied: Genesis 39:1-23; all verses mentioned in the lesson

The *aim* of the lesson: God is honored when His children trust and obey Him–even in testings, temptations and suffering.

What your students should *know*: Just as Joseph suffered, though innocent, so Christ, the spotless innocent Lamb of God suffered.

What your students should *feel*: A desire to please God by being pure, even if it means suffering.

What your students should *do*: Resist the devil and deliberately turn from temptation.

Lesson outline (for the teacher's and students' notebooks):

1. The beloved son becomes a servant (Genesis 39:1; Psalm 40:8; Philippians 2:5-7; Hebrews 12:2).
2. A well-pleasing servant (Genesis 39:2-6; Matthew 3:17; 17:5; John 8:29; 17:4).
3. A tempted servant (Genesis 39:7-12; Matthew 4:1-11).
4. A falsely accused servant (Genesis 39:13-20; Matthew 26:59-61).

The verse to be memorized:

We know that all things work together for good to them that love God. (Romans 8:28a)

NOTE TO THE TEACHER

This volume is a continuation of Volume 4.

Before teaching these lessons, review briefly the first eight incidents in the life of Joseph which picture the Lord Jesus Christ. Show the illustrations and give your students opportunity to explain the likenesses of Joseph and Christ.

In this volume, each likeness of Christ is illustrated on one of the covers.

THE LESSON

Have you ever suffered because of your love for the Lord Jesus? In what way? How did you react? What did you say? What did you do? What did you learn from the experience? (*Teacher:* Encourage group discussion. Your students may wish to list in their notebooks the lessons which others have learned from suffering for Christ's sake.)

Almost every child of God who lives to please his heavenly Father knows what it means to suffer. (See 2 Timothy 3:12.) There are two in the Bible, however, who, though they lived about 1,900 years apart, took their sufferings in the same way. Listen carefully!

Day after day young Joseph trudged along under the hot sun on the road to Egypt. The Bible doesn't tell us what he was thinking, but it could've been something like this: *Why did my brothers throw me in the pit? Why did they sell me to these merchants? I was obeying my father when I went to find them. He wanted to be certain they were all right. Why do they hate me?*

But then, remembering the good things his father had taught him, he stopped thinking and prayed instead. "Dear God, I can't understand why my brothers sold me to these merchants. I don't know why they're taking me to Egypt. But I do know You are watching over me. I know You have all power. You know everything. You have a plan for our family. You are with us wherever we go. And You're watching over me right now. What has happened is Your plan for me. Dear God, please get honor for Yourself from my life."

After praying, Joseph walked with head held high.

1. THE BELOVED SON BECOMES A SERVANT
Genesis 39:1; Psalm 40:8; Philippians 2:5-7; Hebrews 12:2

Show Illustration #1

Arriving in Egypt, the merchants took Joseph to the noisy market where slaves were sold and bought. One shouted, "Who will buy this strong young man? He looks as if he will work hard. He's good enough for the king's household!"

"I'll buy him!" Potiphar announced. (Potiphar was the captain of the king's bodyguard and the chief executioner.) "He's yours!" the merchant declared.

Joseph, the one especially loved of his father, now belonged to someone else. Instead of enjoying the life of a son, he would do the work of a slave. Turning to follow Potiphar, Joseph thought, *I'll probably never see my father again. I loved doing things for him and with him. Now I have to do whatever this owner demands. I'll never have any rights of my own.*

Long years later, the Lord Jesus Christ, God the Son, laid aside all His rights. He had always been with God the Father. Both enjoyed the glorious shining brightness of their home in Heaven. Together they were worshiped by multitudes of angels. But the Lord Jesus, beloved of His Father, willingly left His heavenly home. Coming to earth, He accepted a human body.

Show Illustration #1a

On earth, He who was equal with God did what only a slave would do: He washed the feet of His disciples. Then He died painfully, shamefully on the cross. But He delighted to do this because it was the will of His Father. (See Psalm 40:8; Philippians 2:5-7; Hebrews 12:2.)

2. A WELL-PLEASING SERVANT
Genesis 39:2-6; Matthew 3:17; 17:5; John 8:29; 17:4

When Joseph entered Potiphar's home, he thought, *What a magnificent place! So much marble! So many statues! Such big rooms! And so many slaves! But I can't understand what people are saying. Will I ever be able to speak their language?*

In his heart, Joseph prayed, "Dear God, make me a useful, good servant in this place. Help me to obey my master. Living here is entirely different from life in the simple tents of Jacob my father. This is not the place I would choose to live. But You have allowed this, dear God. So I ask You to help me to honor You among these strangers. I know You will give me the strength for my work. Thank You, dear Lord."

God (who always hears the prayers of His own) heard Joseph's prayers. He blessed Joseph and caused him to succeed in everything he did. (See Genesis 39:2.)

Show Illustration #2

Calling Joseph one day, Potiphar said, "You're different from any servant I've ever had. You work hard. You're honest in all you do. Everything you do goes well. Your God is really blessing you. (See Genesis 39:3.) So I've decided to put you in charge of everything here. You'll oversee the shepherds, the workers in the fields, and the slaves in the house. You will take care of all my business affairs. I know I can trust you."

Joseph was delighted! Immediately he prayed in his heart, saying, "Thank You, dear God, for making me a good servant. Help me to do all my work well so You will be honored."

So Joseph, the one slave who knew the true and living God, was given the highest post. All the workmen knew that Joseph believed in the Lord God. And Potiphar realized that he himself received good things from God because of Joseph. (See Genesis 39:5.)

The Lord Jesus Christ was the Servant of God, His Father. Right here on this wicked earth, Jesus lived to honor God. He could say, "I always do those things which please the Father." (See John 8:29.) And "I have glorified God on earth." (See John 17:4.)

Show Illustration #2a

On two different occasions God the Father opened up Heaven and announced publicly, "This is My Son–the Beloved–in whom I am well pleased." (See Matthew 3:17; 17:5.)

3. A TEMPTED SERVANT
Genesis 39:7-12; Matthew 4:1-11

The years passed and God continued to favor Potiphar's household because of Joseph. Potiphar trusted him. The other slaves respected him. All was going well.

One day Potiphar's wife thought to herself, *Joseph is a nice-looking man. I wish I could be alone with him.* She tried to get him to look at her. To her amazement, Joseph ignored her. When she asked him to make love to her, Joseph was shocked.

Show Illustration #3

"Mrs. Potiphar, you belong to my master," he said firmly. "It would be sinful for me to touch you. Potiphar trusts me completely. How could I do this great wickedness and sin against God?"

Satan hates God, and he hates the family of God, especially those who obey God and honor Him. Satan knew that Joseph trusted God. If Satan could cause Joseph to sin, he could bring dishonor to God. And Joseph's good life would be ruined.

The greater Servant of God, the Lord Jesus Christ, was also tempted by Satan. Right after He was baptized, Jesus went into a desert for 40 days.

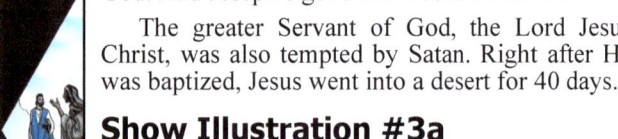

Show Illustration #3a

There Satan tried to persuade Jesus to do as he said. (If Jesus would obey him [Satan], then Jesus would not be able to take the place of sinners on the cross.)

But Jesus deliberately refused to obey Satan. He spoke the Word of God with such force that Satan was defeated. So he left the Lord Jesus alone. (See Matthew 4:1-11.)

Satan still tries to get each one to obey him. He tempts those in the family of God to lie, to steal, to cheat, to gossip, to be unkind. (*Teacher:* Name temptations your students face.)

How can those who trust in Christ refuse to yield to temptations that come every day? The Word of God has the answer: "Give yourself to God. Resist the devil and he will flee from you." (See James 4:7.) Satan will put all kinds of wrong ideas and sinful desires into your heart. But God promises to help you to say "no" to the devil. (See 1 Corinthians 10:13.)

4. A FALSELY ACCUSED SERVANT
Genesis 39:13-20; Matthew 26:59-61

Potiphar's wife usually got what she wanted. Day after day she coaxed Joseph to sin. (See Genesis 39:10.) A time came when no one else was around. She grabbed Joseph by the sleeve and begged him to make love to her.

Joseph jerked away (leaving his coat in Mrs. Potiphar's hand) and dashed outside. "Help! Help!" she screamed. "That Hebrew attacked me!" she lied.

Slaves came running quickly. They could hardly believe her story. They knew Joseph was not that kind of man. But they were only slaves. How could they question their master's wife?

Show Illustration #4

When Potiphar came home, she showed him Joseph's coat. Again she lied, insisting, "Joseph tried to make love to me!"

Potiphar was angry–so angry, that without giving Joseph opportunity to say a word, he threw him into prison.

Why? Why should innocent, honest Joseph suffer like this? Why should he be condemned by the lies of a sinful woman? Why was he not allowed to tell his side of the story? Why should he, who had been faithful, be punished this way?

Show Illustration #4a

Hundreds of years later, the Lord Jesus Christ was also falsely accused. The Jewish leaders searched–without success–for someone to speak against Jesus. Finally they found *two false* witnesses who told lies about Him. (See Matthew 26:59-61.) The people believed their lies rather than the truth spoken by the Son of God. So Jesus was condemned to death.

Is God receiving honor from your life? Do you humble yourself willingly and serve others? Can God say of you, "I am well pleased with this child of Mine"? When you are tempted to do wrong, do you obey God? Do you deliberately turn from the devil? When people lie about you, do you fight back? Or do you trust God to take care of you and your reputation?

List in your notebook whatever testing, tempting or suffering you are having. If God has shown you how you can honor Him, even in these hard places, write that in your notebook. Then we will pray together, asking God to help you live this week in such a way that others will give glory to Him.

Lesson 2
TRIALS IN EGYPT (Part 2)

> **NOTE TO THE TEACHER**
>
> Circumstances should make no difference to the child of God. Since the Lord is always with His own, problems of life can be accepted as a gift from Him. Joseph, even though he was sold into slavery, did not take his eyes from the Lord. Three times in Genesis 39 God records, "And the LORD was with Joseph." Once He says Joseph "was a prosperous man" (v. 2). Twice He adds that the LORD made all that he did to prosper. And God built character into Joseph which few other men in the Bible had. Except for the fact that Joseph had a sin nature, he was a wonderful picture of our Lord. He didn't become bitter when his brothers treated him unkindly. Nor did he allow his time in prison to enslave his soul.
>
> Potiphar saw that the LORD was with Joseph. The prison keeper favored Joseph because the LORD was with him. In the words of the New Testament, Joseph let his light shine, so that men glorified the Father in Heaven. (See Matthew 5:16.) May this be true of your life, teacher!
>
> Before teaching this lesson, you will want to review the four ways in which Joseph pictured Christ according to our last lesson.
>
> 1. Joseph, the beloved son, became a servant in Potiphar's house. Christ, the beloved Son, became a Servant in the world.
> 2. Joseph was well pleasing to Potiphar. Christ was well pleasing to His Father.
> 3. Joseph was tempted to sin by Potiphar's wife. Christ was tempted by Satan.
> 4. Joseph was falsely accused by Potiphar's wife. Christ was falsely accused by Jewish leaders.

Scripture to be studied: Genesis 39:20–40:23; all references mentioned in the lesson.

The *aim* of the lesson: To show that God is in control of everything.

What your students should *know*: God controlled all the circumstances in the lives of Joseph and Jesus Christ.

What your students should *feel*: Gratitude for all that happens–both good and seemingly bad–since God has allowed it.

What your students should *do*: Accept life's problems cheerfully, remembering that God is in control of all things.

Lesson outline for the teacher's and students' notebooks:

1. Punished, though innocent (Genesis 39:20; Psalm 105:17-21; Matthew 27:27-31; Acts 4:26).
2. Respected by government official (Genesis 39:21-23; Mark 15:39).
3. In company with sinful men (Genesis 40:1-4; Isaiah 53:12; Mark 15:27-28).
4. Telling the future beforehand (Genesis 40:5-23; Luke 23:39-43).

The verse to be memorized:

We know that all things work together for good to them that love God. (Romans 8:28a)

THE LESSON

What can you say about your life this past week? Was God with you when bad things happened to you? Is He in control, even in the hard places of life? Can God bless us and make us successful even when everything is going wrong? (*Teacher: Encourage discussion.*)

1. PUNISHED, THOUGH INNOCENT
Genesis 39:20; Psalm 105:17-21; Matthew 27:27-31; Acts 4:26

Show Illustration #5

In prison, Joseph had much time to think. God has not recorded his thoughts for us. But they could've been like this:

If only I could see the sunshine again! Oh, for a breath of fresh air! I wonder what my father is doing at home. Do my brothers ever think about me? Will they ever try to find me? How long will I be in this dark, smelly place? These chains hurt my feet. (See Psalm 105:18.)

Why did I have those wonderful dreams? I thought they were from God. I thought He was showing me that I would rule over others. So did my father. He should have known, for he spent much time talking to God. Did we make a mistake? I tried to be honest. I tried to do what was right. I didn't do anything wrong. But here I am in prison.

Show Illustration #5B

Our Lord Jesus Christ never sinned. He never did one wrong thing. Yet kings and rulers were against Him. (See Acts 4:26.) The Roman soldiers made fun of Him. They slapped Him, spat on Him and put on His head a crown of thorns. Finally they nailed Him to a cross to die. (See Matthew 27:27-31.) Did God know? Did God care? Indeed He did! For this very purpose He had sent His Son to earth. (See John 3:16; 12:27-31.)

The beloved Son of God was perfect in all He did. He didn't deserve to be abused and mistreated. But He, the perfect One, took the punishment for our sins. (See Isaiah 53:3-7.)

2. RESPECTED BY GOVERNMENT OFFICIAL
Genesis 39:21-23; Mark 15:39

God heard Joseph's prayer in prison just as He heard him when he had prayed in Potiphar's house. God helped Joseph to praise Him and honor Him even in that awful place.

The Bible says that when a person lives to please the Lord (as Joseph did), God makes even the enemies of that person to be at peace with him. (See Proverbs 16:7.)

Show Illustration #6

This is exactly what God did for Joseph. The rough, hard keeper of the

– 23 –

prisoners saw that Joseph was a good man who could be trusted. So he put Joseph in charge of all the other prisoners.

Joseph was delighted! Now he had special things to do instead of sitting in chains day and night. Joseph was interested in the other prisoners. He listened with understanding as they told of the wrongs they had done. Day after day Joseph had the opportunity to tell them about the true and living God who loved them. And the Lord was with Joseph. He who controls all things made Joseph successful in everything (Genesis 39:23).

Show Illustration #6B

When the Lord Jesus died on the cross, a Roman military officer was in charge of the crucifixion. God caused this officer, who was an enemy of the Lord, to recognize and believe that Jesus was *different*. He exclaimed, "Truly, this man was a Son of God!" (Mark 15:39).

3. IN COMPANY WITH SINFUL MEN
Genesis 40:1-4; Isaiah 53:12; Mark 15:27-28

One day the prison keeper announced, "Joseph, here are two more prisoners. Take care of them!"

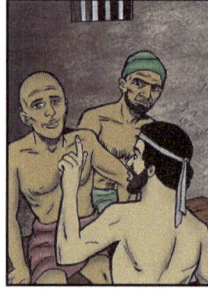

Show Illustration #7

"Who are you and what have you done to be put in here?" Joseph asked.

"I was the king's chief baker," one replied sadly.

The other answered, "I was the chief butler for the king. It was my duty to taste the wine before it was served to him. I had to make certain it was safe for him to drink. The king became angry with both of us. So here we are."

Though there were many prisoners in the dungeon, the Bible carefully mentions these two with whom Joseph was imprisoned.

Show Illustration #7B

This is another picture of the Lord Jesus Christ. He also was in company with two who had done wrong. When He was crucified, there were two other crosses–one on each side of Him. And on those crosses hung two thieves who deserved the punishment they received. (See Mark 15:27-28.) But God was not surprised. Hundreds of years before He had said this is exactly what would happen. (See Isaiah 53:9a, 12.)

4. TELLING THE FUTURE BEFOREHAND
Genesis 40:5-23; Luke 23:39-43

In jail one morning, Joseph asked the butler and baker, "Why are you looking so sad today?"

"We each had a dream last night. We know the dreams mean something. But there's no one to tell us what they mean. This is why we are sad."

"God is the only One who can tell what dreams mean," Joseph explained. "Tell me what you dreamed. I believe God will help me to give you the meaning of what you saw."

Show Illustration #8

So the butler told his dream. "I saw a vine with three branches on it. While I was looking at it, the vine began to bud. Then the buds opened into blossoms. Suddenly there were clusters of ripe grapes on the branches. I held the king's cup in my hand, squeezed the juice into the cup and gave it to the king."

Thoughtfully, Joseph said, "This is what your dream means. In three days, you'll be set free. You will go back to your duty of serving the king. When you are there, please remember me. I did nothing wrong and shouldn't be in this dungeon. Please tell the king I am innocent and ask him to get me out of here."

"Thank you, thank you, Joseph!" the butler exclaimed. "Think of it! I'll soon be out of this filthy jail! I'll surely speak to the king for you. I'll do anything you ask!"

Since the butler's dream had such good meaning, the baker was eager to tell Joseph about his dream. "I had three baskets on my head. In the top basket were all kinds of baked goods for the king. But before I could serve them to him, birds came and ate them."

Joseph spoke thoughtfully, slowly, sadly. "Oh, my friend, your dream is bad news. But I can only tell you what God has shown me. In three days the king will take off your head. Your body will be hanged on a tree for the birds to eat."

Three days later, the butler woke up wondering, *Will my dream come true as God showed Joseph?* The baker's thoughts were quite different. *I hope Joseph was wrong!*

Suddenly the prison doors flung open. The guard announced, "The king's butler and baker are to come to the palace immediately. Follow me!"

The butler followed quickly, his heart pounding. *Joseph was right*, he thought. *I'm free! I will be serving the king again!*

The heavy-hearted baker shuffled along slowly, thinking, *If Joseph was right, this is the last day of my life.*

Down in the dark dungeon, Joseph had hopeful thoughts. *The butler will tell the king about me. Soon his guard will come for me. Then I'll be out of this awful place!*

The butler and baker were led into the palace. There the king was having a big party for all his servants. "Ah, my butler, today is my birthday. To celebrate, I am again making you my chief butler and wine taster," the king announced. "And you, my baker, shall be hanged."

God had perfectly foretold the future through Joseph. What He had said would happen, did happen. God is always in control of everything.

Joseph, who had done nothing wrong, was in jail with two who had done wrong. In the same way, Jesus, the perfect One, hung on the cross between two thieves. One sneered, saying, "So You're the One sent from God, are You? Prove it. Save Yourself and save us, too!" (See Luke 23:39-43.)

The thief on the other cross rebuked him. "Don't you fear God when you are dying? What's the matter with you? We deserve to die. We're being punished because of our crimes. This Man is innocent. He does not deserve to die."

Show Illustration #8B

Turning to Jesus, he said, "Lord, remember me when You come into Your Kingdom."

Jesus answered with this wonderful promise: "Today you will be with me in Paradise."

What God said would happen to the butler and the baker came true. What the Lord Jesus promised the repentant thief came true. Promises He makes to us will come true. To those who place their trust in Him, He promises everlasting life. He vows that those who reject Him will be punished forever. (See John 3:17-18, 36.) Which will you do–trust in Him or reject Him?

What about you who have already placed your trust in the Saviour? Do you understand that God is always in control of everything? Are you thanking Him for everything? (See Philippians 1:12, 20-21, 29;4:11-12; 1 Thessalonians 5:16, 18.)

Everyone who knew Joseph realized that God was with him. Do those with whom you spend your time know that God is with you? Are you really living the kind of life that pleases Him? The Lord Jesus has given us the perfect example. He didn't sin either with His life or His lips. When hateful words were spoken to Him, He didn't say anything hateful in return. He didn't threaten to punish those who caused Him to suffer. He simply committed Himself to God who is in control of everything. (See 1 Peter 2:21-23.) Let us pray asking the Lord to help us accept the problems of life cheerfully, remembering that He has allowed those problems.

Lesson 3
RAISED TO POWER IN EGYPT

Scripture to be studied: Genesis 41; all verses cited in lesson.

The *aim* of the lesson: To lead my students to claim the assurance of eternal life.

What your students should *know*: God has not promised a life without problems here on earth. He has promised His children a glorious life after death.

What your students should *feel*: Joy as they think of that happy future.

What your students should *do*: In gratitude to God for their glorious future, serve Him now this week.

Lesson (outline for the teacher's and students' notebooks):
1. Delivered from prison (Genesis 41:1-13; Matthew 28:1-10).
2. Revealer of secrets and counselor (Genesis 41:14-36; Matthew 13:36-42).
3. Promoted to the highest place (Genesis 41:37-44; Philippians 2:10-11).
4. Saving the people (Genesis 41:45-57; 1 John 5:11-12).

The verse to be memorized:

We know that all things work together for good to them that love God. (Romans 8:28a)

NOTE TO THE TEACHER

Throughout his lifetime, Joseph had great and sudden changes. One day he was his father's favorite son. The next he was sold as a slave. One day he was in charge of Potiphar's household. The next he was chained in prison. One day he was in charge of the baker and butler. The next day he was forgotten by the butler. Then, at long last, because of the lovingkindness of God, he was set free from prison to stand before the king of the greatest nation on earth.

Nothing is beyond the care and power of God. He knows exactly how much each of His children can stand. And He uses each experience of life to develop our character for His purpose.

Review the eight illustrations of Christ in Joseph's life as studied in Lessons #1 and #2 of this volume.

THE LESSON
1. DELIVERED FROM PRISON
Genesis 41:1-13; Matthew 28:1-10

How do you feel when everything goes wrong? Do you think only of the difficulties? Or do you realize that the hard things won't last forever? Can you thank God, knowing He is working *everything* together for your good? (*Teacher:* Encourage discussion. Use Psalm 18:30a and Romans 8:28.)

Two years went by. But the butler was so happy when he got back to work that he *completely forgot* about Joseph.

Poor Joseph! He was still in prison. He *could* have become bitter. Instead he often talked with his heavenly Father. He continually helped the other prisoners.

Then one day the prison door flew open. The guard announced, "Joseph, the king wants you to come to the palace immediately!"

Joseph quickly shaved himself. Changing his clothes, he thought, *Why does the king want me? Did the butler finally remember me after all this time? Will I be set free? Or am I going to be put to death?* Then he prayed, "Dear God, no matter what happens, help me to honor You."

Show Illustration #9

The king wasted no time. "Joseph," he began, "I had a dream last night. None of my wise men are able to tell me what it means. My butler told me that you can tell the meaning of dreams. That is why I have called for you. Tell me what my dream means!"

God had allowed Joseph's brothers to hate him. He had allowed Joseph to be lied about and put in prison. But now God had something else for Joseph. So He gave the king a dream. And He caused all the king's wise men to be puzzled by the meaning.

Likewise, God permitted the Jewish people to hate His Son, Jesus Christ. They arrested Him and nailed Him to a cross. They sealed His dead body in the tomb so no one could steal it.

Show Illustration #9C

But Jesus could not stay dead. (See Acts 2:24.) He is God the Son. The third day He rose again in triumph over the grave! (See Matthew 28:6; I Corinthians 15:55-57.)

2. REVEALER OF SECRETS AND COUNSELOR
Genesis 41:14-36; Matthew 13:36-42

Joseph answered the king saying, "Your majesty, *I* can't tell you the meaning of your dreams. But *God* can. Tell me what you dreamed and God will tell me what it means."

Show Illustration #10

The king said, "In my dream, I was standing by the river. Suddenly, seven fat, healthy-looking cows came up out of the river and ate grass. Then seven skinny, sick-looking cows came up and ate the seven fat cows. But the thin ones remained just as skinny and sick-looking as before.

"I woke up, but soon fell asleep and had another dream. This time I saw seven heads of grain on one stalk. All seven heads were plump and full. But while I was looking at them, seven withered, thin heads of grain swallowed up the plump ones.

"None of my wise men or magicians can tell me the meaning of these dreams. Can you tell me what they mean?"

"Oh, King," said Joseph, "God is warning you of something He's going to do. The next seven years will be good ones. Lots of food will grow. You will have more than enough for your people to eat. After that there will be a dreadful famine for seven years. There will be no grain. The farmers will plant seeds, but there will be no harvest. Everyone will be hungry. But there will be nothing to eat.

"Both your dreams have the same meaning. God showed you the same thing in two dreams. He wants you to know that He *means* what He says. This is going to happen soon."

Clearing his throat, Joseph continued: "Your majesty, I suggest that you choose the wisest man in your kingdom. Put him in charge of all the farmland in Egypt. Have him gather all the extra grain during the next seven years. Keep it securely in the royal storehouses. Then, when there is no grain, your people will have enough food. If you don't do this, they will starve to death."

God chose to make known, through Joseph, what He was going to do. Joseph was simply a messenger of God. Through Joseph, God also made known to the king how his people could escape starvation.

God has made known to us, through the Lord Jesus Christ, things that are going to happen in the future. He warns us that death does not end everything. After death, there is life that *never* ends.

Show Illustration #10C

All who reject the Lord Jesus Christ will be in blackness of darkness, separated from God. They will be sent to a lake of fire which will burn forever. People will gnash their teeth and scream because of the terrible suffering. (See Matthew 13:42; Luke 16:23-24.) God made this place for the devil and his angels. He does not want people to go there. (See 1 Timothy 2:3-4; 2 Peter 3:9; Revelation 20:10-15.)

God tells us in His Word how we can escape this fearful judgment: "Believe on the Lord Jesus Christ [who died on the cross for your sins], and you will be saved." (See Acts 16:31; 1 Corinthians 15:3-4.) This is the only way to be certain of living in Heaven with the Lord.

He is now there preparing beautiful homes for those who have trusted in Him. (See John 14:2.)

3. PROMOTED TO THE HIGHEST PLACE
Genesis 41:37-44; Philippians 2:10-11

The king and his advisors listened carefully to all Joseph told them. The king asked his men, "Who is wise enough to be in charge of our plentiful crops? We must be careful so we have food during the famine. Is there a man who has the Spirit of God in him?"

At that moment the king looked at Joseph and had an idea. "Joseph," he said, "God is with *you*. He has shown you what my dreams mean. He has told you what I should do. There is no one as wise as you. I am now making you ruler over my whole kingdom. Whatever you say will be done. No one, except I, will be over you in the whole land of Egypt!"

What a change! Only a short time before, Joseph was a slave in prison. Now he was the second highest man in all the land! In place of the dirty rags of a prisoner, he was clothed in the king's finest linen. Instead of iron chains binding his feet, he wore a gold chain on his neck. The king's ring was on his finger.

Show Illustration #11

The king gave Joseph a chariot in which to ride. Wherever he went the people shouted: "Kneel down! Kneel down! Here comes Joseph!"

What a beautiful picture of our Lord Jesus Christ! He who died is risen. He lives forevermore. God has exalted Him, raised Him to the highest place. Today He is seated right next to God in Heaven. (See Ephesians 1:21; Revelation 3:21.)

Show Illustration #11C

One day everyone will bow before Him. Each person will admit openly that He is Lord. (See Philippians 2:10-11.)

What a change! The rejected, crucified Saviour is now the Lord in glory. (See Acts 2:32-36; Colossians 1:15-19; Hebrews 2:9.)

4. SAVING THE PEOPLE
Genesis 41:45-57; 1 John 5:11-12

Joseph had a very busy life. Exactly as God had revealed, the farmers harvested much more grain than they needed. Joseph carefully stored the extra crops.

Year after year the supply increased until the grain houses were overflowing. These were happy years for Joseph. He was powerful. The people respected him. The king gave him a lovely wife. And the Lord gave them two sons.

When his first son was born, Joseph named him Manasseh, which means, *made to forget*. "Because," he said, "God has helped me to forget all the years of my trouble." When his second son was born, Joseph named him Ephraim. " 'Ephraim' means *fruitful*," said Joseph. "God has made me fruitful in this land where I came as a sad and lonely slave."

At the end of the seven good years, the land became very dry. The sun shone hot and blistering every day. But there was not a drop of rain. The farmers planted. But they harvested nothing.

"We're hungry!" the people cried. "Our children are hungry. We have nothing to eat!"

The king made a law for all the land: "Go to Joseph. Do whatever he tells you!"

Show Illustration #12

Joseph opened the storehouses and sold grain to all in need. Those in the countries around Egypt had nothing to eat. So they, too, came. And Joseph sold to all.

God, through Joseph, provided food for all who could buy. Not one was turned away. Joseph saved the people from starvation.

Show Illustration #12C

"Place your trust in Jesus!" is God's command to us today. "Now you're bound by the chains of sin. You are in darkness." (See John 3:19-21.) "If you will confess your sins, I will forgive them and set you free. When you truly trust in My Son, you will receive everlasting life." (See 1 John 5:11-12.) "And you will live forever in my beautiful, bright, shining heavenly home." (See Revelation 22:5.)

God also tells us that those in Heaven will serve Him. (See Revelation 22:3.) But between now and then we can serve Him here on earth. He gives us this privilege. (See John 15:16.)

Let us list in our notebooks what we can do for Him today–this week. Then we'll ask God to help us do these things.

(*Teacher:* You may wish to determine beforehand exactly what your students can do for God.)

Lesson 4
JOSEPH AND HIS BROTHERS

Scripture to be studied: Genesis 42:1-50:26

The *aim* of the lesson: To show that everything (good and bad) is working together for the good of the child of God.

What your students should *know*: Even trials caused by those we love are allowed by God for His purpose.

What your students should *feel*: A desire to accept lovingly anything done against them.

What your students should *do*: Thank the Lord for the trials that others have brought into their lives. Determine how they can show their love to those who have caused trials.

Lesson outline (for the teacher's and students' notebooks):

1. Joseph's brothers do not recognize him (Genesis 42:1-38). (Compare John 1:11; 11:47-57.)
2. Joseph tells his brothers who he is (Genesis 43:1–45:8). (Compare Romans 11:26-32.)
3. Joseph sends for his father (Genesis 45:9-28).
4. Joseph's brothers bow before him (Genesis 46:1–50:26. Compare Revelation 5:11-13.)

The verse to be memorized:

We know that all things work together for good to them that love God. (Romans 8:28a)

NOTE TO THE TEACHER

In the life of Joseph we see the hand of God working to accomplish His will. The Bible reports nothing bad about Joseph. He had a sin nature, but there is no record of his yielding to it. No matter what was done to him, Joseph knew God meant it for good (Genesis 50:20). And whatever comes into your life, teacher, is meant for your good to make you like the Lord Jesus Christ. (See Romans 8:28, 29.) Never forget it!

THE LESSON

Has anyone caused something bad to happen to you this week? How did you feel at the time? Did the experience upset you, making you unhappy? *Or* could you say, "Thank You, Lord, for sending this testing to me"? (*Teacher:* Please have your students discuss this.) What do you suppose Joseph (whom we have been studying) said about the trials he had? Listen carefully!

1. JOSEPH'S BROTHERS DO NOT RECOGNIZE HIM
Genesis 42:1-38; John 1:11; 11:47-57

Joseph was 17 years old when his brothers sold him to the merchants on their way to Egypt. Now he was almost 40. And he was still in Egypt.

Back in Canaan, life continued as usual. Jacob, his father, still mourned for Joseph, thinking he was dead. His brothers never could forget their evil deed. (See Genesis 42:21-22.) Each wondered what had happened to their younger brother.

Joseph's brothers married and had children. They kept their flocks and enjoyed the food of their good land. Then, as in Egypt, it stopped raining in Canaan. Seeds were planted, but the tender shoots withered and died under the hot sun. Months went by. Still there was no harvest, no pasture for the flocks.

Finally Jacob called his sons to him. "I have heard there is grain in Egypt," he said. "Unless you go down there and buy some for our family, we will all die."

So Joseph's ten older brothers prepared for the long journey to Egypt. "Benjamin must stay home," their father insisted. "Something awful happened to his brother Joseph. I will take no chance of losing Benjamin." (Benjamin was born to Jacob's beloved wife Rachel just before she died.)

Entering Egypt, each brother wondered about Joseph. Would they see him working in the fields with the slave gangs?

Joseph, who was now the king's assistant, was busy overseeing the selling of grain. All who bought, bowed low before him. This day, he was startled to see his ten brothers bowing down. They did not recognize him, of course. For he wore Egyptian clothing and spoke the Egyptian language.

Show Illustration #13

"Where have you come from?" Joseph demanded roughly.

"We have come from Canaan to buy grain," they replied.

"Aha! You are spies! You have come to see what damage the famine has done in our land!" Joseph said severely.

"No, no! We're not spies. We've come to buy food. We are ten brothers. We're telling the truth. Our father lives in Canaan. We have one younger brother who stayed with him. Our other brother is dead."

Joseph exclaimed, "You're not going to leave Egypt until your younger brother comes here!" Turning to his servants, Joseph ordered, "Put them all in prison!"

Three days later he called for the men. "You can have enough grain for your whole family," he said. "But one of you must wait here in prison. When you return, bring your youngest brother along. Then I'll know whether or not you are telling the truth."

The men talked among themselves in their own language (not knowing Joseph could understand them). One said, "This must be happening to us because of what we did to Joseph long ago." Reuben reminded them, "I warned you. But you would not listen to me. Now we're going to die because of what we did to him." (See Genesis 42:21-23.)

Joseph pointed to Simeon and gave a command to his servant. "Take this one out of my sight." The frightened brothers watched as the rough guard bound Simeon and led him away. Joseph then ordered his servants, "Fill these men's sacks with grain." Secretly he whispered to his servants, "Put the money they pay for the grain back into their sacks. But don't let them know you're doing it."

Joseph's brothers started home with gladness and sadness– glad because they had food for all in their family; sad because their brother was in prison. Stopping for the night, one opened his sack to feed the donkeys. "Look!" he shouted, "my money is in the sack!" The men were terrified. "What has God done to us?" they cried.

Back home, they told Jacob about their unhappy experience with the king's assistant in Egypt. "He accused us of being spies. He kept Simeon in prison. He won't let him come home until he sees Benjamin."

"Never!" Jacob cried. "Benjamin cannot leave! Oh, why is everything against me?"

When the men opened their sacks, they all trembled. For they found all the money they had paid for the grain.

2. JOSEPH TELLS HIS BROTHERS WHO HE IS
Genesis 43:1-45:8; Romans 11:26-32

Weeks went by. Again Jacob and his family had no food. "My sons," Jacob said, "we'll starve unless you go to Egypt and get more grain."

"Father, we can't go unless you allow Benjamin to go with us," Judah said. "I promise to take full responsibility for him."

Sadly, Jacob agreed, saying, "I have no choice. Load your donkeys with gifts for the king's assistant. Take twice as much money, so that you can also pay for the grain you got last time. Oh, that God would hear my prayers and return both Simeon and Benjamin to me!"

In Egypt, Joseph saw his brothers coming. Seeing Benjamin was with them, his heart raced. To his servant he said, "Hurry, prepare a feast! I want these men to eat with me at noon."

When the brothers were led to the house of the king's assistant, they trembled. One decided, "It's because of the money that was in our sacks last time. He'll say we stole it and make us his slaves!"

The men were given water with which to wash. Their donkeys were fed. Simeon was brought out of prison and they were told, "You'll eat with the king's assistant." What a surprise!

When Joseph came in, they gave him their gifts and bowed before him.

Show Illustration #14

Joseph told the men where to sit. Amazingly he seated them in the order of their ages! Their food was served from his own table. He gave Benjamin more than the others.

What a wonderful time they had! But while the brothers were preparing to leave, Joseph whispered something to his servant. "When they pay you, put the money on top of the grain in their sacks. In Benjamin's sack, put my silver cup also."

Happily the brothers set out on their journey home. "How different our trip was this time! Our father will surely be relieved when we get home," they agreed.

Just outside the city, a horseman came from behind them. "Halt!" he ordered. "What do you mean by stealing my master's silver cup? Why would you do such a wicked thing when he has been so kind to you?"

"What are you talking about?" they demanded. "We didn't steal your master's cup. We are honest men. Search our things. The one whose sack has the cup will die. The rest of us will be your slaves forever," they promised.

The messenger replied, "The one whose sack holds the cup will return as a slave. The rest of you may go home."

Alas, the cup was in Benjamin's sack! The brothers tore their clothing in despair. Loading their donkeys again, they returned to the city. They fell to the ground before the king's assistant. Judah spoke for all, saying, "Sir, how can we prove our innocence? God is punishing us for our sins. My father is still sad because he believes his missing son was killed by wild beasts. If we return without Benjamin, our father will die of sorrow. I promised him I would be responsible for Benjamin. Please let me serve as a slave in his place. I dread to think what would happen to our father if Benjamin is not with us."

Joseph saw how much his brothers pitied their father. He saw their kindness toward Benjamin. He saw how sorry they were for their own sins.

Joseph sent all his servants from the room. He cried so loudly he was heard throughout the whole house. Finally he told them, "I am your brother Joseph. Is my father well? You sold me to be a slave into Egypt. But don't be angry with yourselves. *You* didn't send me here. God did. He sent me to keep you alive so that you will become a great nation. Yes, it was God who sent me here, not you!"

Joseph hugged his brothers and all 12 cried happy tears.

3. JOSEPH SENDS FOR HIS FATHER
Genesis 45:9-28

"Hurry home to our father," Joseph told his brothers. "Tell him all that has happened. I'll send wagons to bring him and your families back to Egypt. You will all live in the land of Goshen–the most fertile part of this country. I will take care of you, for there will be five more years of famine. Hurry!"

Show Illustration #15

Crying with joy, Joseph hugged Benjamin and all his other brothers. He surprised them with wonderful gifts. As they left, he called, "Do not quarrel as you go!"

When the brothers got home and told their father the news, he could hardly believe it. "Joseph, my son, is alive!" he cried. "He is the king's assistant! I must see him before I die. But I'm afraid. It is a long trip. Egypt is a foreign land. God wants us here in Canaan."

During the night God spoke to him, saying, "Jacob, do not be afraid to go to Egypt. I will go before you. I will make a great nation from your family in Egypt. Someday I will lead your people back to Canaan."

God kept this promise He made to Jacob. We'll learn *how* He kept it when we study the next Bible book, Exodus.

4. JOSEPH'S BROTHERS BOW BEFORE HIM
Genesis 46:1-50:26; Revelation 5:11-13

When Joseph learned that his father was on his way, Joseph jumped into his chariot and raced to meet him. They fell into each other's arms and cried for a long while.

For 17 happy years, Jacob enjoyed the good things of Egypt. One day he told his sons, "Now I'm going to die. Be sure to bury me in our homeland, Canaan." After blessing each son, he lay back in bed and died.

After they buried him, they returned to Egypt. Joseph's brothers were worried. "Now that Father is dead, Joseph will get even with us. We treated him wickedly. He'll punish us."

Show Illustration #16

Together they went to Joseph's palace. Falling on their faces before him, they begged for forgiveness. "We are your slaves," they said.

Seeing his brothers bowing before him, Joseph remembered the dreams he had when he was young. With great kindness he said, "Don't be afraid of me. You did evil to me, but God turned it into good. He brought me to this place of honor so that I could take care of you and your families."

And for all the rest of his life, Joseph took care of his undeserving brothers and their families.

What about you? How do you act toward those who do unkind things to you? List the names of those unkind people in your notebook. Write down what you believe God wants you to do for them this week, to show them you are not against them. By being kind to those who are unkind toward you, you'll become more and more like the Lord Jesus Christ. (See Romans 8:29.) On a separate piece of paper, write in big letters: GOD MEANT IT FOR GOOD (Genesis 50:20). Place this where you can see it each day. Then, no matter what is done to you, remember the words of Joseph and those of our memory verse: Romans 8:28.

www.ingramcontent.com/pod-product-compliance
Lightning Source LLC
Chambersburg PA
CBHW060801090426
42736CB00002B/117